EQ KILLED THE RADIO STAR

How Emotional Intelligence Can Crush Or Crash Your Organization

ALAN VANDERBURG

Published by Authors Place Press
9885 Wyecliff Drive, Suite 200
Highlands Ranch, CO 80126
AuthorsPlace.com

Manufactured in the United States of America.

ISBN: 978-1-62865-670-1

CONTENTS

SECTION #2

PUTTING EMOTIONAL INTELLIGENCE (EQ)
SKILLS INTO PRACTICE

FORWARD

If you love music then *EQ Killed The Radio Star* is for you! If you love being more effective in your life, then this book is for you! If you love being entertained while learning things that can improve your career, then this book is for you!

Alan has done something remarkable here, tying music and the history of rock bands to bottom line Emotional Intelligence (EQ) insights that are engaging, informative and enlightening. After all, as the research show, 75% of a person's effectiveness in working with others, in living a meaningful, satisfying life, in being a leader, is about how developed she or he is in emotional intelligence. IQ only plays about 25% in this capacity. Alan makes that insight come to life while goes into developing, in having and utilizing great EQ!

Having been a consultant who has worked on bringing EQ insights, awareness and skills to corporations and executives for decades, I had thought I had seen it all. Alan surprised and delighted me by cleverly looking at the impact of EQ on the survival rate of rock bands and tying that into how each of us can be more effective, successful and even joyful in how we work and live. The connections and insights are richly engaging and highly informative.

After all what is the commonality between rock bands and work groups? Who would have made that connection? Alan knows and makes that connection! He does it gently with humor, insight and clear examples. Alan then goes on to show how to build and maintain effective teams using EQ examples from Rock Bands with clear application to business groups and organizations.

How good is your self-awareness? How accurately do you understand how others see you? How effectively can you adapt to changing conditions, situations and differences in people? What is your level of personal mastery when it comes to living authentically and whole heartedly? Can you access the act of courage you need in the right moments at the right times?

How well can you read other people and situations and then bring your best game, your best self forward? Alan's book can help you to improve and become even more proficient in all of those areas by understanding the power of "programming" (unconscious cognition / perceptual patterns) in impacting your thoughts, feelings, behaviors and the results you get in life. He then goes on to show you how to move beyond any self-limiting or perception-altering "program" and take charge of your life.

I highly recommend Alan's book. It is engaging, entertaining and highly educational, offering clear, concrete examples for both understanding and utilizing emotional intelligence insights and skills. He offers ways of communicating, listening and engaging that create positive, reinforcing cycles of good will and stronger, productive relationships. The journey starts with you and doing an honest assessment of your EQ (emotional intelligence). How often have you seen or read about very smart people really screwing up their careers and lives due to a lack of self-control or poor insight or inability to flex and change. After all, even the best super computer is only as good as the software programming that instructs it how to perform. And for us humans, as Alan so effectively outlines, the programming instructions telling us how to use our intellect is emotional intelligence.

Are you ready to be even better, smarter, more insightful and effective in how you run your business, your life? If so, *EQ Killed The Radio Star* is the book to read.

- Robert (Dusty) Staub, Founder of EQIQ,
President of Staub Leadership International
Best selling author of
The Heart of Leadership and *The 7 Acts of Courage*

PREFACE

MY LOVE FOR ALL MUSIC AND THE GENESIS BEHIND THE BOOK

My love for music goes back as far as I can remember. I got my first record player when I was about 5 years old. It was an orange portable record player that I played "*Let's Get Together*" from the Disney movie Parent Trap, over and over again. I loved the guitar in that song. As I grew up I loved all kinds of different music. I was like a sponge, as far as collecting and exploring different music styles. Even before I was a teenager I joined the mail record club; remember those – 13 records for $.01. Well, with shipping and handling it probably was not a great deal, but that is where I purchased some of my first albums from groups such as ELO, Ted Nugent and Journey. As a young teen, I remember going to a garage sale on the next block and buying a boatload of 8 track tapes at a ridiculous bargain. That is where I discovered bands like Yes, Uriah Heap and Robin Trower. I would often ride my bike to the library and file through all the records, looking for cool album covers to check out and take home. I discovered Jethro Tull, Hall and Oats, and one of my favorite guitar players Lee Ritenour. A studio musician who can play just about any type of music around. When I was old enough to drive a car, I got a job at a local restaurant in Tulsa as a busboy. I would save up my tip money and go to the local record store called Dale Bishops Record Alley. Most of their used records were $1 and I loved it. It was there that I purchased some really unusual music like Starz, Brian Brain, and bootleg copies of Led Zeppelin Live. Starship Records and Tapes was another local Tulsa record store that stocked punk music like Black Flag, Dead Kennedy's, the Dead Milkmen, and Suicidal Tenancies. I was all over the music style map. I was a sponge for just about any type and style of music. I remember in high school, I would have a Devo tape in the tape deck, my radio channel on a country station and talking to my friend about a new funk jazz guitar player that I discovered. All my friends would make fun of me, but I loved all kinds of music. For example, I enjoyed country songs like "*The Fireman*" by George Strait, "*School Days*" by jazz funk artist Stanly Clarke, and *"My War"* by the punk band Black Flag.

As most young boys around age 10, I found a band that I thought ruled the world. That band's name was Kiss. My cousin Randy and I would often times dress up in makeup and dark clothes and play some serious tennis racket air guitar. At his house we would jump off of the kitchen counter and spit red ketchup onto newspapers, just like Gene Simmons. Thanks to my Aunt Betty, who supplied us with real clown makeup, we painted our faces and even used Bic lighters to simulate the fire-breathing act that the band would do in their live shows. Was it dangerous? Of course, but we didn't care. We were trying to emulate our heroes from the Kiss albums such as *Love Gun, Dressed to Kill, Kiss Alive, Destroyer*, and *Rock and Roll Over*. Looking back now, I am absolutely amazed that as young boys we had no idea what some of those songs were talking about. We just loved the music, and the look of the band.

Along with Kiss, my cousin Randy and I would explore other rock music as well. I never will forget the first time I heard Rush through a Walkman at my grandmother's house. The drums on *2112* were absolutely incredible. We also discovered some other well-known bands like Cheap Trick, AC/DC, and an obscure band called Angel. The first time I heard Journey *Captured,* was in my cousin's garage playing pool. We were playing *"Line of Fire"* so loud I thought were going to blow the windows off the house.

Along with Kiss, I also listened to some other music that my mother would cringe at. The first time I heard the *Blizzard of Oz* album, by Ozzy Osborne, I thought Randy Rhoads guitar was the most awesome thing I had ever heard. I was so obsessed with Ronnie James Dio and the Black Sabbath album *Heaven and Hell,* that I listened to the album song by song and wrote the words out on a piece of paper and gave it to my cousin Randy as a Christmas present one year. *"Winches Valley"* is still one of my favorite songs on that *Heaven and Hell* album.

The radio was also impactful on my life. I loved to listen to KMOD, KWEN 95 and in Oklahoma City the KATT was the home of rock music when I was a kid. I remember the first time I heard *"Roxanne"* from the Police. I thought it was the coolest song I had ever heard.

One band that absolutely changed my life was U2. When I was 16 years old I bought my first guitar. My mother made great sacrifices financially to pay for me to take guitar lesson and I'll never forget the gift of music that she gave me. Danny Holiday was my first guitar teacher and he was perfect for my wide style of musical tastes. He was a jazz guitarist playing in a country band. Need I say more? He taught me a lot about old 70's music, as well as learning the new style of Christian music that was very popular in the 1980's. Bands like Petra, The Resurrection Band, The 77's, Phil Keaggy, and Sweet Comfort Band were some of the first songs I learned how to play on guitar.

I was not a very good guitar player, so when my friends decided to start a band, I became the singer. We were a local Christian rock and roll band, called

Radiation and we would play cover tunes off of the first two albums from U2. *"Out of Control," "Gloria,"* and *"I Will Follow"* were a part of a very short list of songs we would practice over and over again. The Band also added tunes like *"I Love Your #19"* and *"Alarma"* from one of my favorite Christian rock bands Daniel Amos. Like every young band, we had original tunes like *"X Ray Vision"* and *"Dark Night"* that sounded much like the bands we were listening to at the time. None of these songs were that great, but we did not care. We were a bunch of teenagers in a rock band. We even roped one of my best friends, Warren Chapin, into being our band manager. We had nothing for him to manage, but it was sure awesome to know that we had a band manager if we ever needed one.

One of the funniest moments in the band occurred during a show at our church. My mom had bought a huge parachute from a garage sale in the neighborhood. The band decided to rent a strobe light and we had acquired a large fan from who knows where. You can image what was going through our creative teenage minds. We could tie the parachute to my wrist, turn the strobe light and the fan on and the visual to the audience would be amazing. We did not try this mammoth vision so the first time we did it was during a show. Well, I think you know what happened. The fan did not blow hard enough, and I could not see because the strobe light was shining right in my face. To top it off, the parachute got tangled up in my microphone cord and I was fighting with it for the rest of the show. We never tried that scenario again.

We had a great time with the band. We would crank up the volume and jam as long as we could or until we hit curfew time. We even did a punk version of *"Rudolph the Red Nose Reindeer"* and *"Angels We Have Heard On High Volume"* for a Christmas show. Those were great times. What happened to our band, Radiation, is what happens to most high school bands. We slowly disintegrated. No gigs, no more drive, and we all started to go our separate ways. What is really cool is that our drummer, Brandon Holder, became a professional musician and has been touring with Leon

Russell for several years. He was really good at age 13 and just got better with age.

So, with all this musical influence, it made sense to me as a trainer that I would liken my work to music.

I first heard of EQ from a consultant named Dusty Staub. He presented the Daniel Goldman concept that 75% of a person's success is not due to IQ and their book smarts, but instead, had to do with their Emotional Quotient (EQ). As I continued my formal education in the University of Oklahoma's Masters of Human Relations degree program, I began to really become more intrigued with the concept. I wrote several papers on the subject and began doing public speaking on the topic at conferences and luncheons.

It was at a point where I decided to do some research to evaluate what occurred during the life cycles of some of my favorite rock bands. Could there be a correlation with EQ and their destruction? How would this relate to workgroups and teams in the business world? Would this be a connection that would help people understand the topic better?

I began, for the next several years, continuously reviewing articles, reading books, watching documentary videos, compiling information from the internet, libraries and podcasts on the history of some of my favorite rock bands and how it could relate to the EQ concepts I was learning. I consider myself truly a lifelong student of music history and am at times amazed at how things, like a simple difference of opinion, misunderstanding or lack of commitment, can break up a rock band.

I believed that making the correlation between EQ, rock bands, and business work teams would be a discussion worthy of documentation. As I began adding this discussion to Emotional Intelligence presentations that I was conducting across the county, people seemed to make the same connection that I had made. Rock bands, just like workgroups, are destroyed not by IQ, but by lack of EQ.

This is where the concepts and ideas for the book *EQ Killed The Radio Star* began. So I began to write and put into words what audiences were connecting to during the presentations. I hope this book helps you in some way to find what you do in life and do it to the best of your abilities, to not allow anyone or anything to steal your joy and happiness and to live life to the fullest everyday.

Finally, I want to thank several people for helping me along my journey to understanding and continuously lifelong learning.

On a personal level my mom and my dad and their encouragement to embrace music and life. To my wife Nancy and my two daughters Amber and Ashley, thank you for letting me be the best dad I could be. To my sisters, Cindy, Ruvena and Lisa for their being the best siblings ever.

On the professional side I am forever grateful to Paula Marshall for the opportunity to learn and grow from one of the most gifted business leaders in the world. Lastly I would like to thank Dusty Staub for introducing me to the concepts of Emotional Intelligence.

Me and my first orange record player – Age 5

My Cousin Randy and I dressed up like Kiss when we were about 10 years old

Radiation concert at New Life Center Church – 1984

Left to Right: Mitchell Sand, Alan Vanderburg, Brandon Holder, Steve Patterson

Photo shoot at Joe Lake, Tulsa Oklahoma - 1986

INTRODUCTION

Why are some really smart people not as successful as they could be? Shouldn't people know how to get along with others and treat people with respect? What does emotional intelligence have to do with great rock bands? These are all questions I have been asked over the years.

My journey with emotional intelligence began in 2005, when the manufacturing company that I was working for had a series of what I would call "Company culture wake up calls".

A few leaders in high positions seemed to defy the company culture and mission in a way that lead to their dismissal. This included low EQ behaviors such as discrimination, favoritism, "group think" management structure and the lack of ability to listen and learn. As the leader of the organizational development team and part of the culture keeper team, we were all taken aback at what was uncovered.

We had tried for years to come up with company principles and culture surveys to ensure we were living our mission. We had gone to great lengths to study other company cultures, such as Southwest Airlines which had similar "People focused" cultures that created financially profitable businesses.

The solution for our company culture crisis came in the form of an offsite meeting with the top leadership of the organization. In a short one-hour conversation, led by a consultant named Dusty Staub, Emotional Intelligence became the face of what we were looking for to guide the company culture. The concept and tools were simple to understand. What we did not realize is just how much time it was going to take to implement. Emotional Intelligence is about understanding ourselves first, then applying that learning to others. Dusty told the team that it would take five to seven years to fully implement Emotional Intelligence into the organization. What he really meant is that it would be a lifelong journey of learning for the company.

Fast-forward six years: in 2011 the company had implemented Emotional Intelligence into the company foundations and systems. We used Emotional Intelligence criteria to develop, coach, teach, promote, and hire team members. It was engrained in almost every fiber of the company. That year I decided to attend the ASTD (American Society of Training and Development) International Conference with the sole purpose of collecting, networking, and investigating all the information I could on current trends in the area of Emotional Intelligence. As I began to talk to people and attend breakout sessions, I was amazed at how much information and material was available. I was exposed to brilliant models and research that had been conducted on the subject.

As I began to network and talk to people about what I was "researching" at the conference, I was amazed at the comments I heard. When I told people that the company I worked for had implemented Emotional Intelligence as a foundation of the company for the last six years, I received a very consistent and surprising response. People told me over and over again that they had tried implementing Emotional Intelligence into their organization and that it did not work or they had changed focus. I was surprised and amazed.

It was at that moment I decided I wanted to present at the conference next year. In 2012, I presented at the conference with the title, "Emotional Intelligence: One Company's Seven Year Journey." The simplicity of what we were doing with Emotional Intelligence, along with a little humor, really resonated with the audience.

This essentially began several years of presenting on this topic to a variety of professional groups in Oklahoma, across the US, and even overseas at an HR Conference in Warsaw, Poland.

As a part of those presentations, I began to explore the correlation of Emotional Intelligence effects on my favorite rock bands. How is it similar to individuals and workgroups in the workplace? This particular part of the presentation seemed to resonate with the audience, so I began to refine it over time. The results were that as I continued to discuss in depth the similarities between rock bands and the workplace, there was a connection where the audience remembered, connected and learned from the concept.

Over the past few years there has been extensive research that continues to show that workplaces that focus on improving Emotional Intelligence for individuals and teams have less stress, more collaboration, are more productive and more profitable. There is just something engaging and motivating about working for and with people that have and are seeking to improve their emotional intelligence. Projects seem to flow smoother, are more productive and relationship grow stronger when displays of high emotional intelligence are present in the workplace.

This book is the result of coaching, training, developing and mentoring hundreds of people and teams over the years in the simple tools of Emotional Intelligence.

This documents the simplistic side of Emotional Intelligence. There is absolutely nothing wrong with the 19 areas of emotional intelligence wheel or star or stages that I have seen over the years. I very much appreciate all the recent studies and research that has brought so much light and insight on the subject of Emotional Intelligence. My experience is that many people desire to understand Emotional Intelligence in a way that is understandable, practical, and easy to apply in their lives.

Over the years, I have had the opportunity to learn, grow, teach and coach hundreds of people in the area of Emotional Intelligence or what is sometime referred to as EQ (Emotional Quotient) to all levels and in many different areas of business.

In this book I will present proven tools that will help you improve your Emotional Intelligence. These are skills that have not only helped me, but they have helped the hundreds of other people that I have taught, mentored and coached over the years.

The book is divided into two sections. The first three chapters explore the concept and idea of Emotional Intelligence at a high level. We discuss the idea of choice, the EI formula and the connection between two of my favorite rock bands of all time. The second half of the book presents proven Emotional Intelligence tools that I have used to teach, develop and mentor individuals and teams over the years. The tools internally build on each other, but they are presented in a system because any one of them can be used to increase your emotional intelligence in a variety of situations.

Finally, there are similarities between highly productive work teams and great rock bands that continue to produce decades of amazing music. I ask you to read this book with an open mind and begin to implement these simple skills and modules into your daily life. My hope is that this book will help you effectively grow your emotional intelligence so you can become happier, healthier and more productive.

SECTION #1

UNDERSTANDING EMOTIONAL INTELLIGENCE (EQ)

CHAPTER #1

FREEDOM OF CHOICE

In presenting Emotional Intelligence or Emotional Quotient to others over the years, I always begin the conversation with the idea of freedom of choice. Yes, it's a fun Devo song from the 1970's, but more than that, freedom of choice is a necessary foundation to understanding and comprehending emotional intelligence.

Most people walk around in life saying statements like, "I have to go to work," "I have to pay my bills," or "I have to be friends with that person." The reality is that people have a choice. Let's take for example, showing up for work on time every day. No one has to go to work if they do not want to. There is nothing in your life that prevents you from calling into work and taking the day off. People do it every day. The reality is that if you do not show up for work for a certain number of days, during a certain period of time, according to the attendance policy, you will not have to worry about missing work because you will not have a job. The same is true of buying groceries, spending time with your kids, watching television, or buying life insurance. Communicating to people that they get to choose their behavior every minute of every day has been one of the most powerful gifts that Emotional Intelligence gives to them. When I have presented and discussed this topic with hundreds of people, the light bulb that goes on in people's faces is almost magical. You get to choose how you feel and how you behave. What a gift. There is nothing in this world that "makes" you pay your bills. You can totally choose to not pay your car payment. Again, if you do this for a period of time, you will one day walk outside and find your car not in the driveway because it was repossessed. Whose fault would this be? The bank's? Your neighbor? The repossession company? No. It's yours. Have you ever met someone that arrogantly and confidently says, "I don't pay taxes and I have not in years?" It is true that they may get away with this for a few years, but the time will come when they will get a letter from the federal government and be forced to pay.

So, this idea of choice is a very important basis for the understanding of EQ. Sometimes people say to me, "Well I am the way I am and I really don't want to improve my emotional intelligence." Since I know I can't "change" anyone else's behavior, I say to them, "You don't have to, it's your choice." What I would also ask them is, "Are you happy with the results you are getting in your life?" In life, you can do anything you want, however, results will transpire. This is how people end up in jail, paying back taxes, and getting their cars repossessed. There are always consequences, both positive and negative, that are a result of our choices.

For a period of about 10 years, my wife and I worked with teenagers. The parents would be taken aback when I would tell them that they do not have 100% control over their kids. They would say, "Yes, I do." The reality is all they have is influence. I would have discussions and sessions with the teenagers and tell them, "Do you realize you can do anything you want at your age?" Their eyes would open wide waiting for what I was going to say next. I would tell them, "You can tell your parents you are going to the mall and go to a party instead. What you need to understand is that when your parents catch you, and they will catch you, they will have a very difficult time trusting you again. So, don't blame your parents if they take the car, phone and gaming privileges away because you lied to them. You made the choice."

This also shows up in the workplace. I once had a person I was coaching say to me, "I cannot work with that person." The problem with that statement is the company pays us to work with everyone, so that is not a choice you are going to be able to make at most workplaces. Just think of all the energy people use to avoid and dodge the co-worker that they work right next to. This choice is unproductive to the company and from a career standpoint, unproductive to the individual.

There are so many examples of good choices producing great results. A student makes the choice to study for the test and the result is a higher test score. A co-worker shows up for work every day, works really hard to learn and grow, and build positive healthy relationships with others consistently. It's not surprising to anyone on the team when this co-worker gets the promotion to supervisor.

Viktor Frankl, who wrote the book *Man's Search for Meaning*, is one of my favorite examples of freedom of choice. Viktor was a Jewish psychologist who survived the German concentration camps by choosing love and positivity during the most horrific atrocities ever imagined. In his book he says, "Everything can be taken from a man but one thing: the last of the human freedoms—to choose one's attitude in any given set of circumstances, to choose one's own way." That statement from Viktor Frankl sets the groundwork for the concept that every human has the freedom to choose.

Therefore, when we are talking about EQ, you do not have to be self-aware or self-manage if you do not want to. However, if you tell me and others that you desire to move up in the company and move into a supervisor or manager position, you will certainly not be successful in your goal if you do not pursue higher self-awareness and self-management. Study after study has shown that the higher the level of influence and leadership, the more Emotional Intelligence is needed to be consistently successful. When you choose to continually be disrespectful to your supervisor at work even though you are on an improvement plan for previous disrespectful statements, what do you think will happen? You should not be surprised that you get called in the HR office and lose your job.

Personal responsibility is high EQ and it is displayed by showing up for work on time every day, giving your best at work every day, learning new ways of doing processes, learning how to work with that difficult person because it is expected, and finally, it is about listening to others before offering your overbearing strong opinion. It is possible you could be wrong and learn something new.

Finally, in this area of choice, I want to make sure it is clear that you cannot change anyone's behavior but your own. I often ask in presentations, "How many of you have tried to change someone else: a spouse, a friend, or a relative? Were you successful?" No matter how much we want to think we can, the answer is that we cannot change anyone else. They have to do it for themselves. I have had lively conversations with others about this concept. They say, "I was able to change this other person." The reality is that the person chose to change. This all stems from the idea that we think we have control over others, including co-workers, relatives, or kids. My response is that all we have is influence. We never really have control. Have you ever had a friend say to you, "I am going to marry them and then they will change?" Has that ever worked?

CHAPTER #2

WORST CO-WORKER EVER (EQ/IQ FORMULA)

When speaking on EQ across the country and around the world, I love to ask people to tell me about the worst co-worker or boss they have ever worked with. I am never really surprised at the answers because they are usually very similar. Answers like, "big ego," "know it all," "was disrespectful," "did not listen," "did not know what he was doing and did not want any help" and "creates drama in the workplace." The responses are predictable, however, what is always different is the feeling, emotions, and look on people's face when they talk about this time period of their life. Some people become very emotional and angry just reliving and thinking about what it was like during that time frame in their life. For me, I always comment that one of my worst co-workers was a boss of mine several years ago that was a know-it-all, had a big ego, and if it was not his idea, he would not do it. I spent a lot of time and energy trying to figure out how to present an idea in a way in which they would think it was his. What an emotionally draining process and tough time in my life. It was one of the most disengaging times in my work life. I usually list these "Worst Co-worker Ever" responses on one side of a flip chart. Then, I discuss the idea of IQ on the other side of the page. IQ is simply explained in terms of resume', degrees, certification and book smarts.

What does a resume' tell you about a person? It tells you what skills, education, and projects he worked on. However, it does not tell the hiring team or the hiring manager anything about how or if this person is responsible, productive, or able to get along and fit in with the team they are joining. This is why many companies now require some sort of EQ type analysis, test, or follow up questions as a part of their hiring process.

In the early 1990's Daniel Goleman declared in his book Emotional Intelligence that somewhere around 75% of a person's success has nothing to do with their

IQ credentials, but rather EQ behaviors. In 2005, as a part of my Master's Degree in Human relations, I began to research this formula for validation. Of course, there has been much more research conducted in the last few years, but I was amazed in my research that the lowest I have ever seen the EQ/IQ formula was 65% and it was in the medical field,. This result makes total sense when you think of the fact that a doctor, who is going to do surgery on your knee, better have a lot of IQ skills and ability to perform the surgery. However, it is interesting when I ask a person about a reference for a doctor, they will usually respond by saying something like, "She is a very nice doctor and is a really good surgeon." See how the response was a combination of IQ and EQ? I have had people tell me that they would not go back to a doctor because they felt disrespected or not heard when they were talking to their doctor. Doctors are continually working on bedside manner, which requires listening and empathy, which is absolutely on the EQ side of the formula.

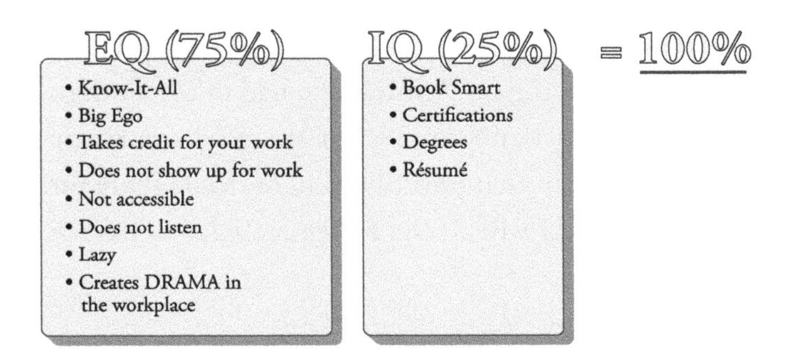

I witnessed a high-level EQ from a doctor several years ago during a very trying time in my family. My mother was having some difficulties so she went in for a series of tests. There we were, my mom, my step dad, my wife, and I in the room, when the doctor came in and said to my mom, "You have stage 4 breast cancer." It hit all of us like a ton of bricks right to the chest. In that moment, what I experienced was indescribable. What did the doctor do? She was calm and allowed the information that was just communicated to sink in. Then, she did something that was incredibly high EQ. She was with our family in that room for 30 to 45 minutes. She would make a statement and then, she would pause and ask, "What questions do you have?" She would lay out options, our next steps, and then she would pause and ask again, "What other questions do you have?" Surely she had other work to do and other patients to see, but she used amazingly high EQ skills in that critical moment, to be there for our family, and I will always be appreciative to her for doing that.

On the other end of the spectrum, the highest EQ/IQ formula statistic I found in my research is not from a formal research study but rather from a personal finance talk show host named Dave Ramsey. When coaching guests on his daily radio show, I have heard Dave state on multiple occasions that personal finance is 80 to 90 percent behavior, which is EQ, and only about 10 percent IQ or head knowledge. Simple personal finance is easy to explain by showing a financial "T" account. The math on personal finance is taught in grade school. The answer to personal financial is "Don't spend more than you make."

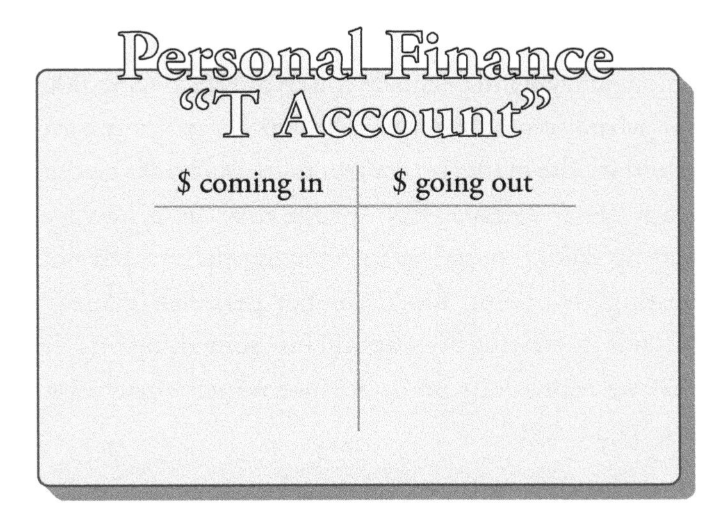

Dave Ramsey spends three hours every weekday taking calls from individuals who are having financial problems and his solution can be summed up in one statement, "Don't spend more than you make." It does not matter if you make a million dollars a year or $10 an hour, you cannot spend more than you make or you will have personal financial difficulties. This is how athletes and famous musicians go bankrupt. They sign a contract for 10 million dollars and spend 10 million +1. Personal finance is not an IQ issue; it is however, an emotional intelligence issue.

This is why it is so difficult when you have a car salesman trying to persuade you to buy a new $35,000 car when you only make $30,000 a year. You can't afford it. The math (IQ) makes no sense, however, our emotions and desire (EQ) for the new car, is how we end up talking ourselves into buying the car. I'm not beating anyone up for his or her personal finances, but it is interesting how we will buy something on sale that we really don't need, because we tell ourselves it is a "good deal."

The EQ formula is so simple we have known about it since we were in grade school. One of my favorite books is called, *All I Really Need to Know I Learned in Kindergarten* by Robert Fulghum. The name of that book is funny, but so true. We discovered low EQ for the first time in grade school on the playground. When we think about the school bully, he didn't have many friends, were angry, and went around the playground beating people up. Much like the worst boss, the bully was self-absorbed and did not really care about anyone but himself. Just to be clear, beating up other kids on the playground is low EQ and the results on the playground culture can cause lasting damage. There is not much difference between some of the behaviors and thought processes of the grade school playground bully and those of our worse bosses ever. They are disrespectful, selfish, and have big egos that make fun of and put others down in order to prop themselves up. This is low EQ behavior.

When I am discussing the EQ formula with groups, at this point I like to get back to a positive by asking the questions, "Tell me about your best boss ever? What made them the best boss ever?" It is amazing to feel the positive energy come back in the room as people talk about great times in their life working for the best boss ever. On many occasions people have discussed how their best boss always encouraged them, believed in them and inspired them to do things they never thought possible. Best bosses who positively challenged them to accomplish personal and professional goals that seemed impossible. It is interesting that I very rarely hear someone say, "They were the smartest person I have ever meet." When I do hear that response I ask them, "What made them the smartest person?" I always get the comment back, "They listened and learned and that is how they became so smart." So the smartest boss ever used EQ skills such as respect and listening to increase their IQ. Interesting.

I think it is interesting to look at the difference between the best boss and the worst boss. The best boss focuses on others, while the worst boss or co-worker focuses on themselves. I always make a point to coach supervisors or managers to be aware of how their actions positively or negatively impact not only the people that work for them, but how often employees bring work events home to their family and friends. There is a lot of talk these days about engagement in the workplace. In simplistic terms, low EQ management results in low engagement and probably high turnover, while high EQ management results in highly productive, engaged and loyal team members.

CHAPTER #3

EMOTIONAL INTELLIGENCE AND THE EFFECTS ON GREAT ROCK BANDS

I have been a music lover ever since I can remember. I recall when I was five or six years old sitting on the floor board of the back seat of my Dad's 1972 Dodge Cornett (yeah we really did not wear seat belts back then), listening to the songs on the AM radio. I distinctly remember songs like *Maggie May* by Rod Steward, *Crocodile Rock* by Elton John, *Frankenstein* by Edgar Winter and Cher's *Half Breed* blaring through the speaker on the front dashboard. My Dad raised us on all kinds of music from country, top 40, oldies, classic rock, and even disco. So I also remember some John Denver, Bee Gees, and Tony Orlando and Dawn. It is amazing how we remember specific points in time like that.

When I started learning and working with Emotional Intelligence in 2005, I began to make connections to various things in my life, such as movies, television shows, and music. Since I had read several books and watched multiple biographies on music stars, it only made sense to begin to make the connection between my favorite bands and the low EQ behavior that lead to short lived careers, tragic endings, and sometimes unrepairable relationships. It is absolutely true that some of my favorite bands are no longer together because of low EQ.

I have always been fascinated by the history of rock bands. How they formed, the rise to stardom, and the "luck" factor of being in the right place at the right time. In my music collection, I have bands you probably have never heard of that are just as talented and produced incredible music, but never made it to popularity. The grind of the rock star lifestyle is rewarding and quite challenging. Big egos, too much fame, too much money, and the hard life of rock and roll took a toll on many of my favorite rock bands. The roller coaster ride of many of the one hit wonder bands even led to a popular movie by Tom Hanks in the 1990's, called *That Thing You Do*. The story of a band that rose to fame very quickly all to have it implode during a national television appearance at the height of their fame. They were truly the one hit wonders.

As I began to research some of my favorite rock bands in terms of EQ and success or failure, I began to become curious as to how some bands like Rush from Canada, could stay together for years through fame, fortune, and tragedy. And yet, other bands like Pink Floyd, Styx or Van Halen (twice) had incredible success and very ugly breakups. I was speechless in 2014, when KISS was inducted into the Rock and Roll Hall of Fame and could not get along enough to play together for one special night at the induction ceremonies. They had been through so much together in the 1970's rising up from obscurity, to one of the most marketable bands in history. What was the reason for why they could not play together at the induction ceremony? Differences, pride, past disagreements and money. All things EQ related, not IQ related.

This story and others about my favorite rock bands, always makes me curious to learn, read, and watch the history of bands. What I discovered and began to research was the amazing similarities between two of my favorite bands, U2 and The Beatles.

U2 was formed in 1976 when the band members met in high school. They started playing together before some of the band members even knew how to play their instruments. This is one of the reasons why they have such a unique sound. U2 released their first album "Boy" in 1980. Over their career, U2 has released a total of 12 studio albums from 1980 to 2009 and sold over 150 million albums in their 35+ year career. They were inducted into the Hall of Fame in 2005 with an incredible list of accomplishments.

Of course, not everything has been easy. The band has had to work through fame, fortune, and even "spiritual differences" over the years. Not only is the band committed to each other, they are committed to those around them. According to the book *U2 Show* by Diana Scrimgeour, U2 has had many of the same stage crew since 1983. U2 believed and was committed to those around them and they sent them to training, etc., so today they can put on stadium shows that are truly amazing.

When it comes to Emotional Intelligence, I believe the band U2 shows some of the best characteristics of high EQ behavior. Just think about it, the same four individuals have been in the same band for over 30 years and they still like creating, touring and working together. Their ability to balance all the activities of one of the world biggest rock acts is one of the main reasons why I believe they have been so successful over the decades. Yes, they have the money and the record sales to call the shots, but it is not often that a huge band like U2 has the self-control to sustain the rock-star lifestyle together for so long. Self-management has been shown over the years in the way they balance touring, creating new music, social causes and their personal life. Have you ever noticed that U2 will go on a world tour for a year and then you will not hear from them for 6 months to a year. Then they will release an album and after that you will not hear from them for a year. I do not know if this is calculated, but as far as work-life balance, they may have the best "Self-Management" of a team I have ever seen in the music business.

Often during EQ presentations, I will ask the audiences, "Who is the bass player and the drummer for U2?" In most cases, there will be a silence in the audience. The answer is Larry Mullen and Adam Clayton. My next question is, "How is it that Larry and Adam do not get jealous of the lead singer and front man Bono?" Over the years, Bono seems to be in the news quite often with his various humanitarian efforts and political views. Because of this, Bono is certainly the most recognized band member of the foursome. I find it interesting that the other band members do not get jealous or have a problem with the fame discrepancies. U2 Band members seem to know their role and are comfortable with it. In a workplace setting, the characteristics of the band members of U2 would be the perfect workgroup to produce incredible results. Alone they may not be the greatest musicians, but together they are committed to each other and they understand how to be an effective team member or in this case, band member.

In comparison, one of my other favorite bands of all time is the The Beatles. What an incredible, creative, and masterful array of musicians. Their roller coaster ride of a career began around 1960 and ended in 1970. The first three years were spent paying their dues in clubs around Liverpool, England. Then, in late 1963, the band exploded on the music scene all over the world. They are the number one selling recording artist, topping Elvis at number two, of all time with over one billion records sold and seventy-two songs in the top 100 hits. Interestingly enough, The Beatles recorded 12 studio albums, almost the same number as U2. The difference between U2 and the The Beatles is that they recorded close to the same number of studio records, but the The Beatles did it in a space of about 6 years. Four of the most talented musicians ever put together in a rock band, collaboratively created all this music in a very short period of time.

Their catapultic rise to success was unprecedented through the 1960's. Unfortunately, and for many different reasons, The Beatles did not have the ability to control all the demands that were put on the band. They were on a six-year barrage of touring, appearances, movies and constant pressure to write and record music. It is interesting to watch some of the early black and white videos and how excited and brotherly they were during those early years. They were having fun, living, and creating what would become the "Rock Star" dream of most musicians. The fact that they were putting out albums approximately every 6 months and touring incisively from 1964 to 1967 was amazing. Yes, they were driven and had incredible chemistry, but someone somewhere should have asked, "Can they sustain this?" From an Emotional Intelligence aspect, their pace could not be sustained. It is the reason why in the workplace, we have a weekend. We need a break. The Beatles, for six years straight did not have a break to relax, reflect, and revive. I believe one of the reasons why some in the band turned to transcendental meditation was to get away from the craziness of the rock star lifestyle. I am not downplaying the success The Beatles had at all, however, I am presenting the idea that if you picked your closest three friends and stuck all of you in a similar situation, you would not be friends at the end of this 6-year experiment.

I am not comparing U2 with the The Beatles as far as success and accomplishments. What I am suggesting is that we can learn from the different approaches that each band took along the way. U2 seems to have found a successful balanced formula for long-term success which has served them well. The Beatles on the other hand took a path that required an unsustainable amount of commitment, time, and energy. A case could also be made that all four Beatles were wildly successful after The Beatles broke up. Paul McCartney sold more than 100 million records.

It is true that throughout the years after 1970, members of The Beatles have collaborated on different works. Ringo and George Harrison joining forces in 1972 to raise money for the refugees of Bangladesh and Paul and Ringo joined George Harrison to record the song *All Those Years Ago,* which paid tribute to John Lennon after his death. After the roller coaster ride of The Beatles, it was difficult for all four to collaborate together after such an ugly breakup that was described as feeling like a divorce.

True, Paul McCartney was very successful in the 1970's with his band Wings, but the reality is that none of the The Beatles were as successful in their solo careers as they were with the The Beatles, because there was only one The Beatles.

CHAPTER #4

COMMONALITIES BETWEEN ROCK BANDS AND WORKGROUPS

What do rock bands and workgroups in the workplace have in common? As I continue to work with developing and coaching individuals and teams, I am absolutely convinced there are key connections that can be learned in the area of emotional intelligence.

Think of some of the most effective work teams you have been a part of. Why were they productive and successful? When I ask this question, people usually say things like, "We worked together well" or "We got the project done and it was fun." Neither of those statements has to do with IQ, but rather EQ. Think about the most dysfunctional team you have ever been a part of. When I ask people about this, I usually get responses like, "It was an awful working environment" or, "We did not work together." Again, these statements have to do with EQ, not IQ.

I have said for years that it is not the work that gets done, or in the rock band scenario that the music gets recorded, but rather it is how the work gets done and what the ramifications are. Is the workgroup or rock band stronger or weaker in their relationships with one another? In effective workgroups, the relationships are strong and friendships last for years. On the other hand, ineffective teams and the drama that ensues can have major impacts on friendships and working relationships for years.

Think of it this way, when a team is put together at work, what do we look for? We often look for IQ skills, such as engineering, accounting, project management, product knowledge, six sigma certifications, etc. When a rock band is forming, what are the band members looking for? Who can play the various instruments like the drums, the guitar, the bass, and who can sing. My question to you is why do most teams in the workplace fail? Often times, it is the lack of Emotional Intelligence. They can't get along, there is disrespect for each other's talents, there are big egos, and maybe even some jealously along the way. This is not any different than when a rock band decides to break up. Common themes of my favorite rock bands breaking up include, lack of self-management – alcohol or drugs, ego thinking, such as "I can do better going solo," creative differences, and even disputes over money and credit for song writing. It is true, sometimes people leave rock bands or business workgroups because they need a fresh new perspective on things. In the rock world however, it is rare that a member of a successful rock band leaves and they become more famous or sell more records.

As I have presented this topic over the years, someone will occasionally come up to me and give me a name of a band member that has been more successful going solo. I like this because it tells me that people are really thinking about the concept I am trying to convey. It is true that Sting and Michael McDonald have been much more successful after leaving The Police and The Doobie Brothers. But for every one of the successful solo breakaways there are hundreds more that aren't successful, such as David Lee Roth of Van Halen, Steve Perry of Journey or one of the most painful for me, the Kiss solo albums.

The bottom line is that most rock bands and workgroups are put together because of their IQ, but fall apart or are not nearly as effective in the workplace because of low Emotional Intelligence.

There is no doubt, as I have presented the EQ/IQ model over the years, that people have connected their life experience, both in a positive and a not so positive way.

Now the question becomes what if we could help people develop and improve their emotional intelligence so there would be less drama, more personal responsibility for work groups, and more productivity?

CHAPTER #5

KEYS TO BUILDING AND MAINTAINING EFFECTIVE TEAMS

The question is how can we build a successful, effective, sustainable workgroup, or referring to the title of this book, a rock band? The answer seems simple, by following the 75/25 EQ/IQ formulas for success. It is absolutely true that IQ is necessary for success. Just like the example of the doctor operating on my knee, we need individuals in our workgroups to be knowledgeable. But more importantly, we need individuals to continually work on increasing their Emotional Intelligence skills.

EQ is not about being perfect, because we are all human and make mistakes. We all know those around us who are truly seeking to increase their effectiveness in Emotional Intelligence.

The key to increasing our Emotional Intelligence begins with us, the person in the mirror. Just like we discussed earlier in the book, it is much more productive to take personal responsibility for ourselves, because we can't change anyone else's behavior except our own.

There are six key skills that must be nurtured and encouraged every day to increase your Emotional Intelligence. The six key skills are:

1. Understanding how your programming gets results (both good or bad).
2. Understanding your self-awareness and your self-management.
3. The concept of listening to learn (from yourself and others).
4. Understanding your fight or flight preference.
5. Understanding what is in your circle of positive impact and what is not.

6. Using the concept of intent, behavior, and results to have meaningful conversations with others.

We will explore and discuss these six Emotional Intelligence areas in detail in the remaining sections of this book.

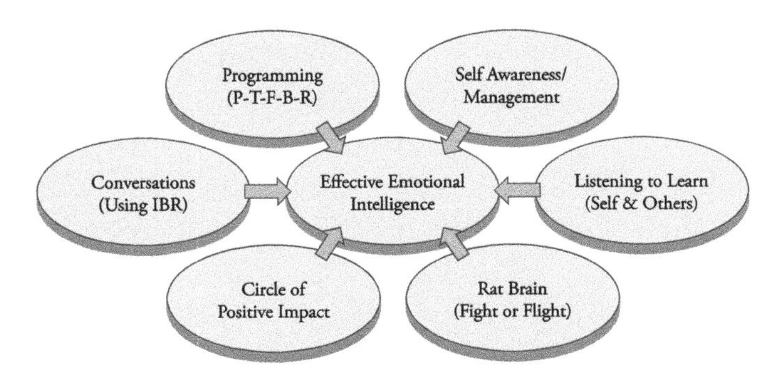

SECTION #2

PUTTING EMOTIONAL INTELLIGENCE (EQ) SKILLS INTO PRACTICE

CHAPTER #6

PROGRAMMING (THE FIRST KEY SKILL)

Programming - understanding how your programming gets results (both good or bad).

The first exposure I had to programming was from my EQ mentor Dusty Staub. He began to explain how programming, and sometimes deep programming is tied to the choices we make. These choices we make either produce a result we don't like and we get upset, mad, or frustrated, or our choices get us the results we were looking for so we continue to do them. It's our choice that produces the results.

Our programming comes from what we've seen, experienced, and been told during our lives. It can be as simple as where we grew up, where we went on vacation as a child, what we have seen on television or through media, or what we have been told about another individual. Sometimes we have programming that we are not even aware exist because we have not discovered it yet.

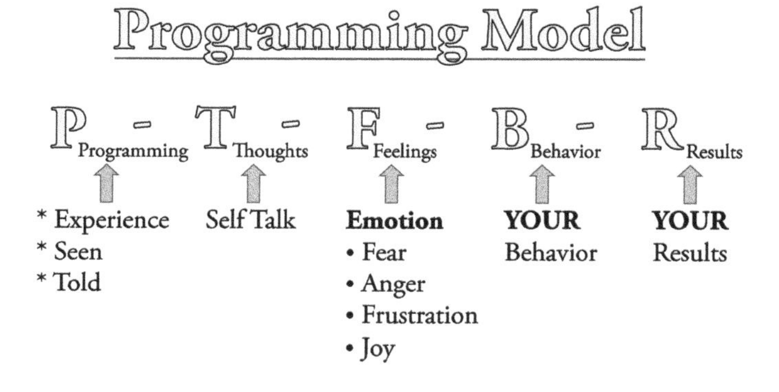

This programming drives us into a thinking process and "Self-Talk." Self-talk can be very effective or very destructive depending on how we use it. If you ask a professional NBA basketball player how he is talking to himself before he shoots, he will probably say something like, "Take a deep breath, calm down, you can make this shot." This is called positive self-talk and the "positive thinkers" understand and make this a key component of their training and teachings.

From our thoughts and self-talk come our feelings about a situation or a person. Our feelings are where emotions come from. The feelings of fear, confidence, excitement, happiness, and sadness all reside in this window.

Our programming drives our thoughts, which drive our feelings, which then drive our behavior. As discussed in the opening chapter, you own your behavior, not anyone else's. When you decide to drive 15 miles an hour over the speed limit and get pulled over by a police officer, whose fault is it? The police officer's? No, that would be your fault. And the result of the situation is a $250 fine, a court date, and your insurance rates go up. Is this the result we wanted? If not, we need to go back into the programming model and explore.

In the speeding ticket scenario, what happened? Our experience is that we have never had a speeding ticket, so we talk ourselves into saying, "I won't get pulled over." We feel so confident that our behavior is to drive 15 miles over the speed limit and the result is that we get pulled over and get a ticket.

What is interesting is that because of the ticket, our programming (experience) changes. So, when you drive off from the police officer, your self-talk changes to, “I will drive the speed limit from now on because I don’t want another ticket.” By the way, if your self-talking is, “It was the police officer’s fault” that you received a ticket, that is a waste of energy and focusing on the wrong area. The result will probably be future continued speeding behavior, which will result in more tickets. The question is, how many traffic tickets will it take for your programming to change? Is it one, two, ten tickets or is it going to take your license being suspended? The choice is up to you.

Who owns your behavior? You. So, if you like the results you are getting, then keep using the same programming, thoughts, feelings and behavior.

For years one of my good friends, Mike Harris and I would go around the country talking to audiences about the programming model and the link to diversity. The programming model seemed to be an easy tool that resonated with people when discussing the differences between individuals. I would use this model as the opening to the Diversity Management class when I was teaching at a local college. The reactions and responses to the discussion would often times leave students and audience members in a "Wow" state because of the clarity and the awareness that was gained.

The model is simple. Suppose I were to show you a picture of a person with a tattoo and ask, "What do you think about this person?" I have asked this question over the years to hundreds of people during EQ training sessions. Participants would respond in a multitude of ways and with various comments. The point being that individuals' answers are based on the variation in their programming. It is truly based on people's experience, what they have seen and what they have been told. From your programming about people who have tattoos, you will have a thought and a feeling about a person you meet with tattoos. This will affect your behavior, whether you talk to the person with the tattoo or not. Your behavior and actions toward this person will result in you having a relationship with a person who has a tattoo or not. So why is this so important?

In a hiring and selection situation, it could mean the difference between whether you respect the person or not, what type of questions you ask them and ultimately if you hire the person or not. This is not about judging you on how you are programmed and telling you to change. I cannot tell you what your programming is; only you know that. I do not know if it is helping you or hurting you with the results you are getting. I do believe however, that the workplace and the world would be a better place if each one of us were to positively change our self-talk toward the differences in others. Embracing differences, such as diversity of thought, how others problem solve, how others think, and respecting other human beings is a powerful positive behavior we should all consider.

The thing I love most about the programming model is that it can be used to teach all ages. Whether it is a student studying for a test, going into a job interview, or dealing with a difficult co-worker, programming can and does help people behave differently and get more effective results. When we continually work on our understanding of our programming, how we think using positive self-talk, how we feel, how we behave, and ultimately the results that we get in our lives, we live a more enriched life and improve our emotional intelligence skills.

CHAPTER #7

EQ SKILLS – UNDERSTANDING YOUR SELF-AWARENESS AND SELF-MANAGEMENT

The second EQ key to success is increasing self-awareness and more effective self-management. As I have coached others over the years, the first area I focus on is self-awareness. Why? Because as I coach others, I really want to know if the person I am coaching is aware of their strengths and opportunities. The more they are aware, the more open to coaching and discussion they are, which leads to improvement.

If I am coaching, the first question I ask someone who is in a performance situation, is “Why are you here?” The reason I ask that is to see what the individual’s response will be. If their response is, “I don’t know” then I stop there and begin to explore further with them to uncover the reason. Their response tells me that they are not aware, either by denial or victim of why they are having performance issues. I really believe that we owe it to co-workers to respectfully tell the truth so they can increase their self-awareness and ultimately manage themselves in a more productive way.

Increasing self-awareness is not as easy as it may seem. Often times we are blinded by our own shortcomings and need the input of others. All of us should seek to have a small team of a few trusted friends or advisors that we can bounce ideas and thoughts off of, thus increasing our self-awareness.

When we increase our self-awareness, we can then begin to manage ourselves in a more productive way. When we focus on learning more about ourselves, something seems to happen where we automatically become more self-aware.

I recently had an opportunity to attend a multi-day training certification session in Chicago with about 30 colleges. After dinner on the second night, we all went on a walk and I began to talk to a person whom I had not met before and she told me in a very caring way, that I was not someone she would care to hang out with because I was too positive and too outgoing. Believe it or not, I was not angry when she told me this. I was actually fascinated that she felt so comfortable sharing this insight with me. No one had ever told me that. I had always assumed everyone liked me and wanted to be around me. Later that evening, I had a similar conversation with another individual who was attending the sessions and he told me that within the first 10 minutes of meeting me, he wanted to hang out with me as much as possible during the week. So the question is, what do you do with self-awareness input that is conflicting like that? I was so thankful that I was a part of that experience and insight for myself. My self-awareness increased immensely because I now realize that not everyone will like or embrace my positive, outgoing personality. What I also realized is that others may really need my positive outgoing personality. What a gift both of those individuals gave me that night in Chicago by giving me insights that increased my self-awareness.

Some people would not have embraced the input I received that night. To be honest, it is difficult for me sometimes to receive feedback. I have to trust the people who give me feedback and be in the right frame of mind. It is true that I have been given feedback in the past from people who had hidden agendas or arterial motives. It is not easy to not become angry, defensive and hurt by the feedback. When we do truly seek out this feedback, it can absolutely increase our self-awareness that leads to better self-management. The best way I know to receive feedback is to proactively ask and productively receive input from other people. This will help raise self-awareness and keep us learning, growing and helping create strategies to manage ourselves better.

CHAPTER #8

LISTENING TO LEARN

Listening to learn is one of the hardest EQ modules for me to speak, coach and train on. It's difficult because it seems so simple, yet sometimes very difficult to do. But yet, listening is so important that I often say that if you cannot listen to learn well, you are going to have a difficult time effectively using any other EQ skills. Just like the person who gave me insights into my lively and over the top positive personality, listening is absolutely key to improving your emotional intelligence.

Becoming a more effective listener is much more difficult today than in the past because there are so many distractions in our day-to-day world. A recent study published by Deloitte in 2015, revealed that the average person in the United States checks their phone

46 times per day. Another often-quoted study from many years ago claims we are exposed to over 5,000 media advisements a day. I don't know if that is true, but the reality is that the number of advertisements that beg for our attention daily is astronomical and more than we are probably aware of.

Think of the last time you truly tried to focus and listen to a spouse, a child or a friend during a conversation. What was going on inside your head while you were trying to listen? If you are like me, I would imagine there was a lot of self-talk and difficulty focusing on the content and what the other person was saying.

In my opinion, Self-talk is the single most difficult barrier to listening to learn. We talk to ourselves thousands of times during the day and it is no different when others are talking to us.

Most typical conversations in our daily lives usually go something like this: the other person is talking to us and they say something that triggers a thought we have. The trigger might be something as simple as a discussion about our hobby, money, family, work, or vacation. The self-talk becomes so loud that we are waiting for the other person to finish the sentence so we can respond with our thought. We are so anxious to speak our thoughts that we don't even hear the last part of the other person's sentence. Self-talk triggers thoughts such as, "Wonder where we are going to dinner," "I wonder if we are going to be able to pay our bills," "That was a great movie, but I have seen an even better one." This kind of self-talk distracts us from hearing some and even all of what the other person is trying to communicate to us. I would challenge you, next time you're in a conversation, notice how many conversations are going on in your head as the other person is talking. It is amazing. Our mind is so powerful it can create multiple self-talk sentences in a row. Unfortunately for the other person talking to us, our self-talk is so loud we sometimes have no idea what the other person is saying.

The idea that a person can effectively multi-task, especially in an area like listening and thinking, is almost impossible. There has been many research articles written on the subject of multi-tasking. In Psychology Today (May 12, 2014), Dr. Nancy K. Napier wrote an article titled "The Myth of Multitasking." She discusses the idea that our brains are not really multi-tasking, but rather switching tracks between tasks.

Have you ever been talking to someone on the phone, while doing something else around the house? At some point during the conversation the person on the other lines says, "Can you tell me what I just said?" This is when you realize you are busted and have no idea what was going on in the conversation. You were not truly listening. The result is the other person can feel like they are not important, not respected, and sometimes hurt. Relationships with others are the number one reason why listening to learn is such an important Emotional Intelligence tool.

I will admit that the idea of listening to learn is not easy, but it is possible to improve. If you are looking for a magic trick here, I don't have one. The only advice I can give revolves around focusing and increasing awareness. In our previous chapter, we discuss you owning your behavior, so here we go.

I think the “Why” listen to learn, also needs to be explored. Just think about how you felt the last time you were truly listened to. For leaders, co-workers, and family members, it is imperative to your EQ effectiveness to take a hard look at controlling our self-talk during conversations with others. If you are in a leadership position, listening could be the most productive, profitable, and engaging work you do for the people that work for you. If you are a parent, managing your self-talk and listening to learn could be the best thing you could do to build and maintain a positive relationship with your children.

Listening to learn is hard. Managing your self-talk, while listening to others, takes focus and an incredibly high self-awareness. However, the results of increasing your listening to learn EQ skills will positively impact the relationships with everyone in your life.

CHAPTER #9

RAT BRAIN (FIGHT OR FLIGHT)

The next step to effective Emotional Intelligence is understanding what we will call Rat Brain. Rat Brain in the most simplistic terms is the human reaction all humans have when we feel threatened or attacked. Why is this important to effective emotional intelligence? It is important to understand how we behave in certain circumstances and instances. Do we flight (walk away) or do we fight (attack back). We usually lean towards one reaction over the other. However, the reality is that most of us use both depending on the situation.

Think about a situation where you felt threatened or attacked verbally. Understanding what was occurring before, during and after the situation occurred is important. How was your heart rate, high or low? What was your self-talk? What were you feeling? What were your actions and behaviors? And the big question is what was the result and impact on the relationship and the issue presented?

One of the best examples I like to use to explain Rat Brain is road rage. Someone cuts you off on a busy highway and they did not even bother to signal. At this point in time you have a choice to make. You could stomp on the gas and go after the person, or you could calmly let off the gas and let the situation subside.

This exact scenario happened to me many years ago during the festive Christmas holiday season. My wife and my two small children decided to go shopping all day at one of the busiest malls in town. I was driving our little Geo Metro…you know the car that looked like a tinker toy or go-cart on wheels. Seriously, the doors on this car could not have been more than 6-inches thick, but it got incredible gas mileage. We were turning onto the highway and suddenly, out of nowhere, the car next to us decided to cut into our lane. In that moment, I immediately went to the Rat Brain "fight" mode. I stomped on the gas and away we went very fast down the highway, 85 miles an hour showing on the speedometer, and yes, the Geo Metro can go that fast. We caught up with the other car and I gave them "The look." What do you think was going on in the other person's car? The female passenger in the other car was yelling at the male driver just like my wife was yelling at me. Now, as you're reading this you are probably saying to yourself, "I would never do that." Ok, but think about the last time you really got mad. Where you really in control? Think about how many IQ points are lowered when we are in a Rat Brain state. We say and behave in a way that, on paper and IQ wise, makes no sense whatsoever. The bottom line: in my road rage scenario I put my wife, my kids, myself, and everyone else on the highway in danger because of my actions. The possibility that we could have had a wreck in that dinky Geo Metro car and died, escalated dramatically because of my behavior. As I realized what was happening, my foot began to let slowly off the gas and we let the other car go down the highway. I will never forget that experience and how truly dangerous of a situation I put my family in.

Verbal forms of Rat Brain "fight" can also be seen in conversations with others. Have you ever been so mad talking to another person that you did not remember what you said? This state is unproductive and can be dangerous, destructive and even unhealthy. Think about how high your blood pressure is during the conversation. How long did it take for your heart rate to return to normal?

There is also the other side of Rat Brain that is just as dangerous, but sometimes not as easy to identify. This is called the "flight" mode. It shows up, for example, when a person becomes silent or quiet in a business meeting after some intense discussion. The person is in Rat Brain and is not engaged in the conversation. This can be just as destructive because the person is not engaged and may not feel valued or heard. This state is also not productive to the situation and can harm the relationship.

Rat Brain is a part of human nature, but learning how to manage it is absolutely necessary if you are a leader. The first step in coaching others to manage Rat Brain is to become more aware of what triggers Rat

Brain for you. Certain words or circumstances can cause people to go into the Rat Brain state. Identifying what those triggers are beforehand is critical. Take a couple of minutes and list some circumstances or words that get your heart rate up.

Preventing Rat Brain is almost impossible, but managing it is crucial to successfully improving your EQ skills. As a leader, external displays of Rat Brain can be career damaging and cause people to lose trust and confidence in their leader. Managing Rat Brain effectively requires quick identification of triggers and the ability to reframe the situation using positive self-talk.

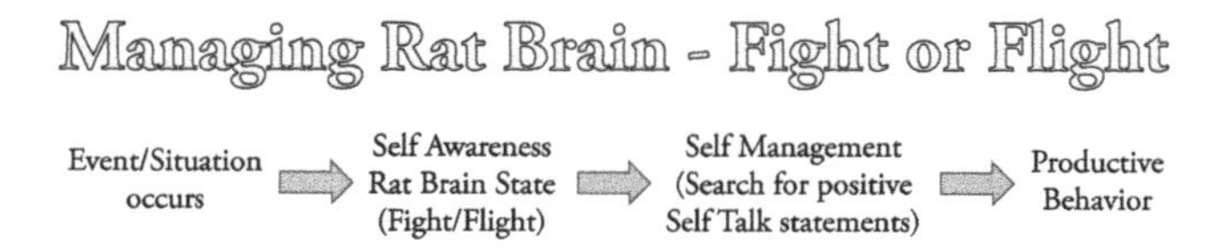

A few years ago, I received a bill in the mail from the local cable company. Using my programming knowledge, I knew why my bill had increased 23%. You see, I had signed up for six months of free premium channels, in which they told me I could call them and cancel when the promotion was over. So, I called customer service to rectify the situation. After waiting on hold for several minutes, a woman came on the line. I explained to her the situation and waited a few seconds. Her response was not what I was expecting. She said, "Actually, the reason why your bill is 23% higher is because we raised prices across the board to all of our customers." At that point I had a choice. Yes, I was doing some serious self-talk. It is true that I briefly visited the idea of going into Rat Brain and going off on the customer service representative. However, if I would have started yelling at her, she would have hung up on me and I would not have got the results I was looking for, which was a lower cable bill.

As I took a deep breath, I began searching for positive self-talk statements, rather than negative statements. I said to myself, "This is not her fault." I remained calm and said to her, "I know you were not in the room when this decision was made. I feel really bad for you because I bet you've had a pretty rough day with all the negative people calling in and yelling at you because their cable bill was raised significantly. Is it possible we could do something to prevent my cable bill from going up so much?" At that moment, the person on the other line took a deep breath and said, "I'll see what I can do." After 25 minutes and multiple transfers to other departments, I got transferred to what they called "The Legacy Department" for long standing customers. I was able to get my bill reduced from a 23% hike to 10%. I did not get all the results I wanted, but because I managed my Rat Brain in that moment, I was satisfied with the result.

Whether at home or in the workplace, it is important to improve your Emotional Intelligence by understanding and managing your Rat Brain in a way that is productive, healthy, and has a positive impact on others. The steps to increase self-awareness and use productive self-talk to create more effective self-management are beneficial to you and those around you.

CHAPTER #10

CIRCLE OF POSITIVE IMPACT

Circle of Positive Impact is the fifth step to increasing your Emotional Intelligence. The first time I heard about the concept of Circle of Positive Impact was several years ago when I read the book, *Seven Habits of Highly Effective People* by Stephen Covey. The basic premise Stephen Covey discussed is that around 85% of what people worry about every day, they don't have any control over. Understanding how much you worry about things you cannot control and seeking solutions that positively impact the situation is a key component to increasing your emotional intelligence.

A person only has so much energy in a day and if they waste it worrying about things they can't control, then there is no energy left to focus on positively searching for solutions and actions that can reduce the worry.

Think of all the things people worry about that they have no control over: politics, the stock market, a new job, management decisions, or the weather. It is entirely possible that a person could spend 24 hours a day, seven days a week worrying about situation after situation that they have no control over. It does not have to be that way.

It actually can paralyze some people and begin to spin them further and further away from searching for solutions. The way people behave when they feel they have no control over their lives is fascinating. We all have ups and downs in life and I will tell you that I have had many situations where I felt like I had no control. I would encourage you to live life every day, look for ways to keep moving forward and commit to not getting stuck in negative situations, concern and worry.

I love to ask people this question, "What are some things you worry about?" The typical responses are areas like work, family, money, health, and even the weather. It is absolutely imperative that you be honest with yourself about what you truly are worried about. Denial, hiding, or lying to yourself about what you are truly worried about will not allow you to move forward with solutions. Moving from worry to creating possibilities ultimately reduces worry and stress. In coaching hundreds of people over the years, I will tell you that I have met a few people that do not desire to stop worrying about their circumstances or situations. They seem to want the stress and cannot see any other way out. Just like we cannot "Make" people come to work, we cannot "Make" people stop worrying or stressing. It is their choice. I do not have the answer as to why, but I have met a few people that seem to want to hold on to their victim worry mentality.

We can influence in some ways, but we cannot make others behave in a different way. The tool for moving from worry is simple, but must be done and owned by each individual.

Below is a simple 5-step process that helps us move from Concern and Worry, to a productive healthy Circle of Positive Impact.

Moving from Concern and Worry to Circle of Positive Impact

Step #1	List the circumstance or situation that you are really worried about.
Step #2	On a scale of 1-5, rate how much you worry about the situation or circumstance. A 1 rating means you worry about it a lot. How much control do I have over the circumstance or situation? (Full, Partial, or None)
Step #3	Answer the question, "What could I do to make the situation or circumstance better?"
Step #4	Pick the top three areas and create an action with a timeline.
Step #5	Positive Impact - Do what you say you are going to do.

These steps are not meant to be difficult, on the other hand, they are meant to be so easy that you don't have to even write them down.

Let's take a simple example and walk through the steps. Step #1: I am worried about running out of gas in my car and the red light coming on. Step #2: on a scale of 1-5, it is a 1 (very important) because I only have a few more miles before I completely run out of gas. Step #3: "What could I do to make the situation or circumstance better?" I could stop at the next gas station, even if the price of gas is $.20 higher than other gas stations. Step #4: create an action with a timeline. I could look on my cell phone maps app for the nearest gas station. Step #5: Positive Impact: I drive to the nearest gas station and put gas in my car. Now you are probably thinking this was a very generic example and wouldn't everybody stop to get gas? I would ask you to look around next time you're driving and see how many people have run out of gas when faced with this same situation. They made the choice to ignore the low fuel indicators and now they are really worried about being late to where they are going.

The Circle of Positive Impact process can also be used in situations such as having a difficult conversation with a friend, co-worker or neighbor, doing a financial budget, or paying your bills on time.

One of my favorite stories to tell is one about my mother. Several years ago, I went across town to visit my mom at her home. I walked in her house and said,

"How are you doing, Mom?" She said she was doing much better. She began to tell me that she had written a letter to the editor of the local newspaper. She was so happy she had done this. The funny thing is I really don't remember what her point or the situation was, I just remember thinking, "This is great, Mom is not going to worry about this anymore."

You know as well as I do that the newspaper was not going to print her letter, or post it on the Internet, I'm not even sure they ever read it. That's not the point. The point is that my Mom was concerned about something that was written in the paper, she recognized she was concerned about it, she made a plan to write a letter to the editor, and afterward she did not have to worry about it anymore. The positive impact my mother made was not to anyone else but herself. She can't control what was written in the newspaper, but she can control how much energy she spends worrying about it. She ultimately created an action that removed her concerns.

One caution in this Emotional Intelligence section of Circle of Positive Impact is to make sure your goal is not to change anyone else's behavior. As previously discussed, if your action plan is to change someone else's behavior, you are going to be sadly disappointed in the results of your plan because they may or may not choose to change.

I have seen these five steps of Circle of Positive Impact truly change people's lives. The steps are not difficult to understand, however, just like most emotional intelligence tools, using them will take time and focused effort. Not using this tool can keep you frustrated, feeling helpless and remaining in a victim mentality state. On the other hand, if you use this tool effectively, you will worry less, feel more in control of your life and have more positive energy to put into productive healthy activities.

CHAPTER #11

CONVERSATIONS USING IBR

The ability to effectively communicate is one of the most difficult Emotional Intelligent skills to master. I have seen people worry, struggle and even ignore difficult conversations which needed to occur. Effective conversations in difficult situations can be scary, terrifying and sometimes feel like a waste of time. Sometimes even casual conversations can be difficult when we do not have a plan.

In coaching people over the years, conversations with others are usually the first area that people want to improve their emotional intelligence. To have an effective conversation with someone, requires effective use of all of the other EQ modules: programming, self-awareness/management, listening to learn, Rat Brain, and circle of positive impact.

Conversations are not difficult until they are. Most of our lives revolve around conversations that are not that big of a deal and don't really require a lot of thought or planning. But for those conversations that are important, that we worry about, that steal our joy and our happiness, there is a simple EQ tool you can use. Unfortunately, people often avoid the conversations that need to occur the most. I have coached many individuals that have avoided conversations that needed to occur around disagreements or negative relationships. Sometimes this situation between two individuals has been going on for years. Why would someone avoid or have bitter feelings towards a co-worker for something that occurred 10 years ago? I don't really know, but I will tell you that I have met people in this situation.

Does a critical conversation need planning? Yes. However, I do not believe it needs to be complicated.

Conversation Using IBR

RESULT: What will be the result of the conversation?

↑

BEHAVIOR: What and how are you going to communicate?

↑

INTENT: What is your intent in having the conversation?

Using the three simple steps of the IBR (Intent, Behavior, Result) model in a conversation can move the relationship with a co-worker, friend or neighbor to a different state and create new possibilities. Creating an IBR for any conversation takes a little bit of time and planning and the results can be miraculous.

The first step in creating a conversation is to ask yourself, "What is my intent?" Positive intentions such as, "I want to tell them some information and get their input" or "I would like to truly understand their viewpoint" are productive and healthy in creating an effective conversation. However, intents such as, "I want to make them look bad" or "I am going to tell them the way it really is" are in the Rat Brain fight state of mind and you are not ready at this moment to have the conversation. Being in a Rat Brain or victim state, does not mean you get to pass and never have a conversation. It means you need to work on your emotions to get to a state where you can have an effective conversation. As we discussed in the previous chapter on Circle of Positive Impact, if the situation is worrying you or bothering you, then the conversation needs to happen. IBR begins by building a plan and scoping out a timeframe for the conversation to occur. In coaching many people over the years, I have been amazed at how many times people have used their programming to talk themselves out of having a conversation, when it really needed to occur. Ignoring a conversation that needs to happen will most likely end up with the relationship or situation getting worse and not better. In these situations, something needs to happen and that something is a conversation using IBR (Intent, Behavior, Result).

Once you have identified what your intent in having the conversation is, step #2 is to think about your behavior. What and how do you want to communicate your message, concern or issue? Use the EQ skill of listening to learn and self-talk to gain insight into how you might want to plan out the words you want to communicate. If your self-talk is so loud that you can't effectively say what you want to say, then you will have difficulty using the words you want to use. If your behavior plan is to do all the talking, then how are you going to listen and understand their point of view? If you don't care about their point of view, then your intent is not positive.

The last step is to ask this question, "What will be the result and impact on myself and others after I have this conversation?" The answer could be less stress for you, better working relationship with a co-worker or even a better understanding of your teenage son or daughter. Use your self-talk to think about all the positives of having this conversation. You are saying to yourself, yeah but what if it does not work?

What are the negatives of having a conversation using IBR? Well, I am not going to tell you everything will be perfect and the stars will align and everything will be OK. Remember, we discussed that we cannot control other people's behavior and that is certainly true in a conversation. The reality is we don't know until we have the conversation. I will say that it is going to be better for you to have the conversation than to not have the conversation. Let's say that you are worried about a situation with a co-worker and you decide to have a conversation. The result is that the two of you still do not agree on how to solve the situation. My contention is that having the conversation will move the relationship to a different state and that is better than not having the conversation at all. Stop worrying about it. You may want to come back with another conversation and keep building the relationship stronger. If the co-worker does not participate in the process, then at some point you may have to say to yourself, "I've done all I can do, I respect them and will work with them and this is where this relationship is at this point."

I believe we use IBR (Intent, Behavior, Result) in our everyday interactions with family, friends, neighbors, and co-workers. Think about what happens when we go to a next-door neighbor's garage sale. Your intent is to buy a piece of furniture for your living room at a fair price and retain the currently strong relationship that you have with your neighbor. Your behavior is respectful, your tone of voice is calm and you ask the neighbor, “Would you take 20% less for this piece of furniture?” The neighbor says, “How about 15%?” You say, “OK” and the result is that you completed the transaction with the neighbor and your relationship is still positive.

Now, let’s just say your neighbor in this scenario says to you, “I cannot take less than what is marked.” If at any time you do not get a result you want in any conversation, you have a choice. Those choices focus back on the IBR model and your intentions and your behavior. Positive IBR conversations are not about manipulation, which over time can lead to trust issues being brought into the relationship. Instead, your intention in this scenario was to get the furniture at a fair price and keep the relationship with the neighbor strong. Therefore, yelling at them would not be an appropriate behavior because it does not match your intentions. However, you could say something like, “Well I am interested in buying it, could you tell me more about it?" or "Maybe we will come back later in the day." Now the tone of voice in either one of these questions is critical to meeting your intent. Both of these questions show respect and keep with your intention of a healthy relationship with the neighbor. Bottom line is that if you are not getting the results you want using the IBR conversation tool, then you need to go back and evaluate your intentions and your behavior.

These types of conversations occur multiple times during the course of a typical day at work and at home. I believe if we begin to become more self-aware about the IBR (Intent, Behavior, Result) model, then we will become even more effective in getting the results we want.

CHAPTER #12

LIVING AN EFFECTIVE EQ LIFE

Living an effective EQ life does not mean perfection. We are all human and will make mistakes. Understanding these EQ tools can increase our effectiveness and productivity in our lives at work and at home. Growing our emotional intelligence everyday causes us to live life with a healthier perspective and more productive outcomes. By focusing on ourself instead of others, it brings a sort of self-satisfaction that we are in control of our behavior and the results of our behavior. Understanding our programming and how it affects our behavior is difficult and deep work. Getting feedback from others that increases our self-awareness is sometimes not the easiest behavior to embrace, but it helps us learn and grow. Think of all the positives to increasing our emotional intelligence on a daily basis? If we manage ourselves around our co-workers, friends, and family, is that not a more effective, productive, and happier life. Being more aware of our Rat Brain triggers and our fight or flight reaction cannot only keep us from looking like an idiot in front of others, but it can also lower our blood pressure and increase relationship with others.

How can that be a bad thing? Reducing stress by using our energy for more productive behavior, instead of worrying about things we cannot control, can guide us to new careers, relationships, and discoveries. Finally, using the IBR (Intent, Behavior, Result) module to have productive, effective conversations with others, can help us building long lasting relationships with others and help us achieve the positive results we are seeking. Using all of these effective EQ tools can increase the quality of life for you and for those around you.

If you are a leader at any level of an organization, higher EQ skills are becoming more and more of a requirement for success. The ability to guide instead of command, the ability to encourage instead of berate and the ability to lead instead of manipulate are all skills that organizations are looking for more and more. If you want an engaging workgroup team that will follow your lead, these EQ tools can help you identify and maintain effective leadership skills and transfer them to those you lead.

Finally, I will give you one last word on living an effective EQ life. The best way I know how to increase your emotional intelligence is to do it. Practice these skills every day. Look for examples in your life, on television, and when you go to the movies. Notice when EQ skills are positively present and when they are not. See and understand the results and evaluate how you might have handled the situation differently using the EQ modules and tools. Many of us seek a better, healthier, and more gratifying life. These EQ skills will help all of us on this journey we call life.

Lightning Source UK Ltd.
Milton Keynes UK
UKHW021430130720
366459UK00010B/450